A LOUISIANA BAYOU CHISTMAS WITH PAPA ODIS

Norma J Graves

ISBN-10: 1533510377
ISBN-13: 978-1533510372

DEDICATION

This coloring book is dedicated to my children and grandchildren.

Artist's Note

A LOUISIANA BAYOU CHISTMAS WITH PAPA ODIS was written to bring joy to my children's families, and now we offer it to the world to bring joy to all families. It is best when colored together, as the joy it brings is in the time spent with those you love.

A LOUISIANA BAYOU CHISTMAS WITH PAPA ODIS

DOWN HERE IN LOUISIANA, CHISTMAS TIME IS A TIME TO SEE MAGIC EVERYWHERE. ALL YOU HAVE TO DO IS LOOK FOR IT. SINCE THE SWAMP IS ONE OF THE BEST PLACES TO SEE IT, I TOOK OFF DOWN TO IT ONE DAY AROULD CHISTMAS TIME IN HOPES OF SEEING SOMETHING OF THIS MAGIC.

.

WHAT DO YOU KNOW? I RUN INTO A FAMILY OF ALLIGATORS ON A PICNIC.   IT WAS OLD PAPA ODIS AND MAMA NET , AND THEY WERE TALKING ABOUT WHAT TO GET THEIR BABY BOY, JOHN, AND HIS FRIENDS FOR CHIRSTMAS.

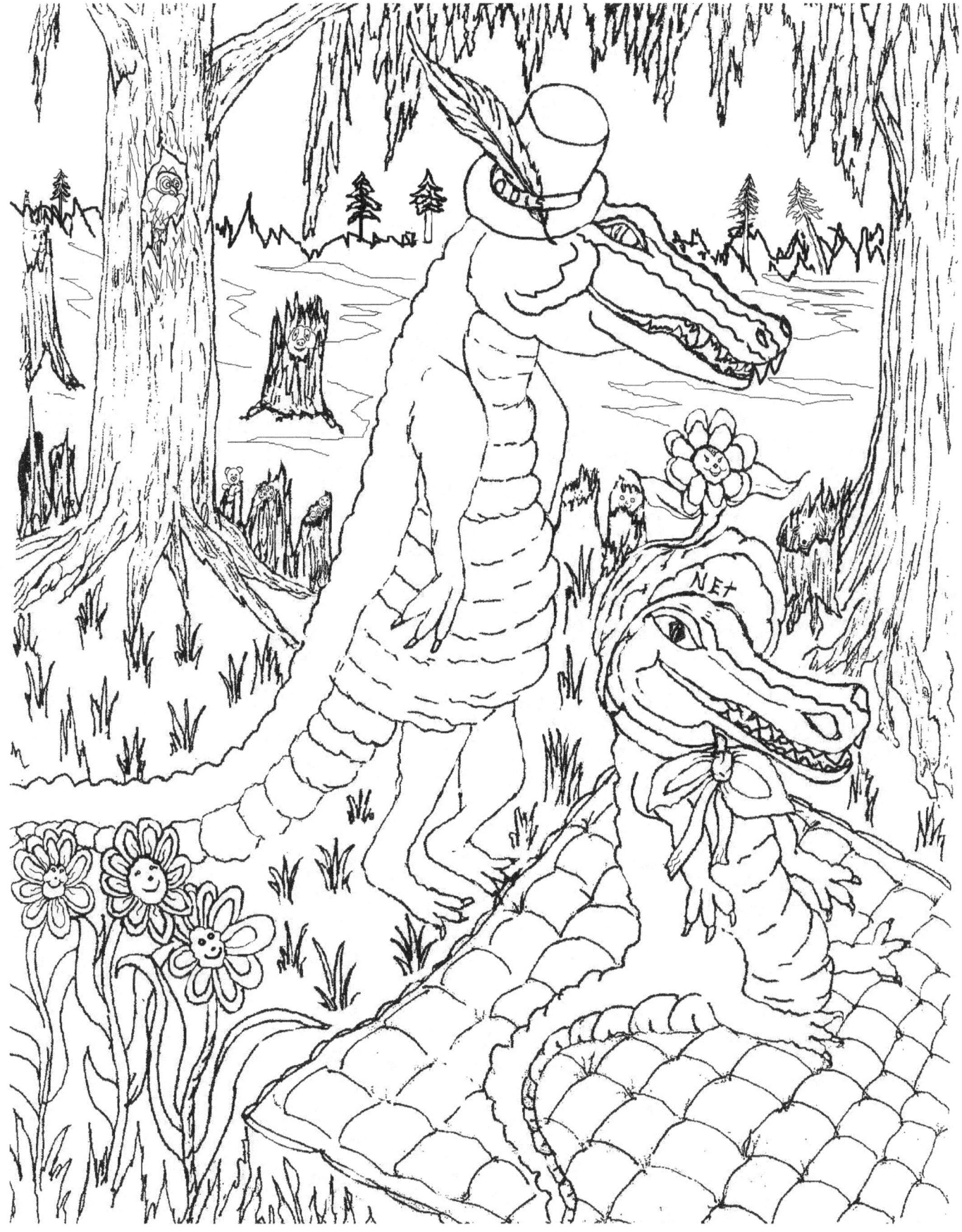

I ASKED THEM, "DO YOU HAVE VERY MANY FRIENDS IN THE SWAMP?" PAPA ODIS SAID, "YES, ONE OF OUR BEST FRIENDS IS NAMED MAYBELLE, AND SOME SAY SHE HAS LOTS OF MAGIC AROULD HE, BUT I DO NOT KNOW ABOUT THAT. I DO KNOW SHE IS A BOTTLE COLLECTOR AND SHE HAS A DAUGHTER NAMED MELAND. NOW THAT THERE MELAND, I KNOW SHE HAS MAGIC BECAUSE SHE IS A SHIFT CHANGER. SHE CAN TURN HERSSELF INTO ALL KINDS OF THINGS. ONE OF THE CREATURES SHE LIKES BEST TO TURN INTO MOST IS A SNAKE SO HER MOTHER CAN USE HER AS A WALKING CANE."

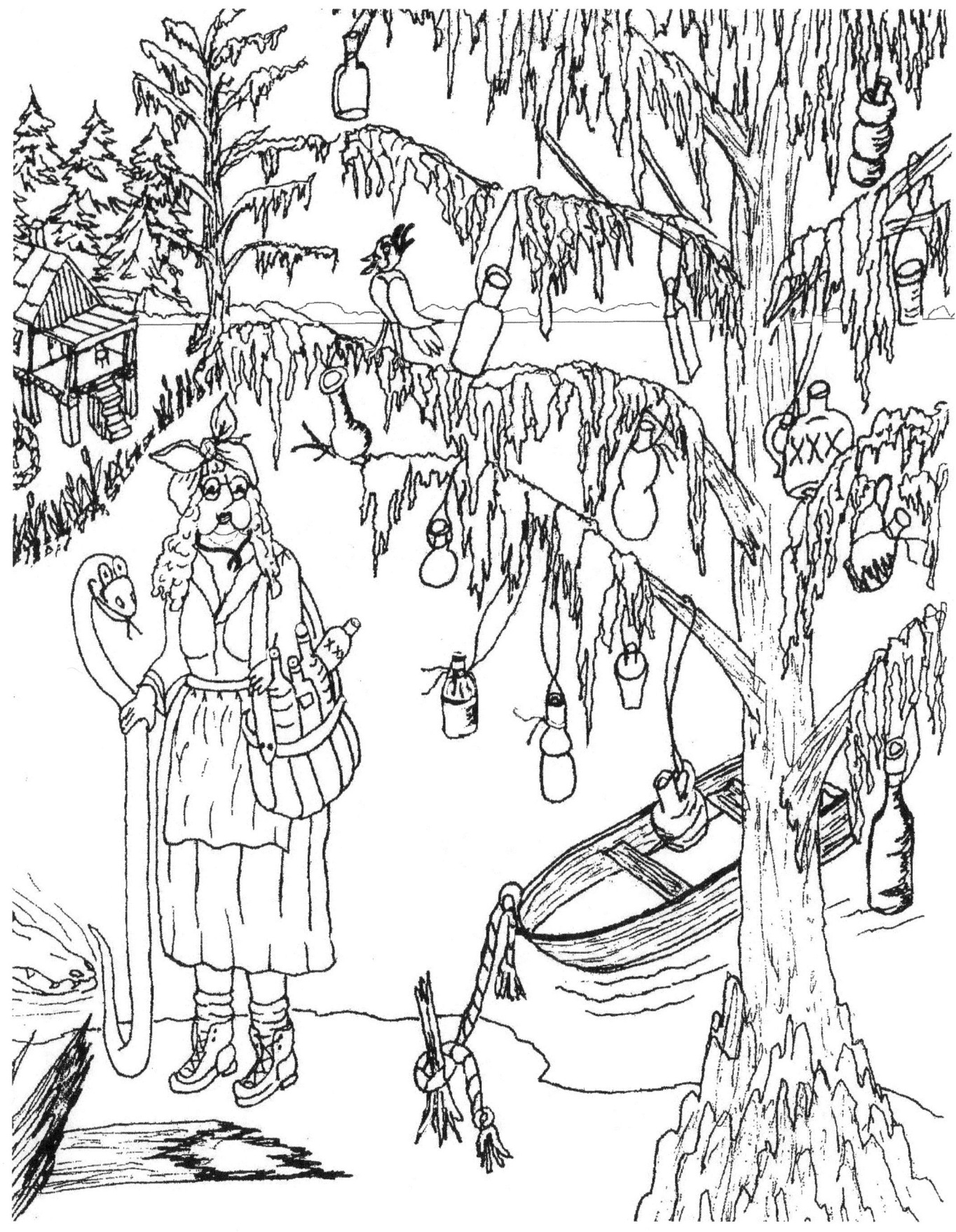

WHEN MELAND WAS NOT USING HER MAGIC, SHE WAS JUST A HAPPY LITTLE GIRL THAT LOVED TO FISH AND PLAY IN THE SWAMP.

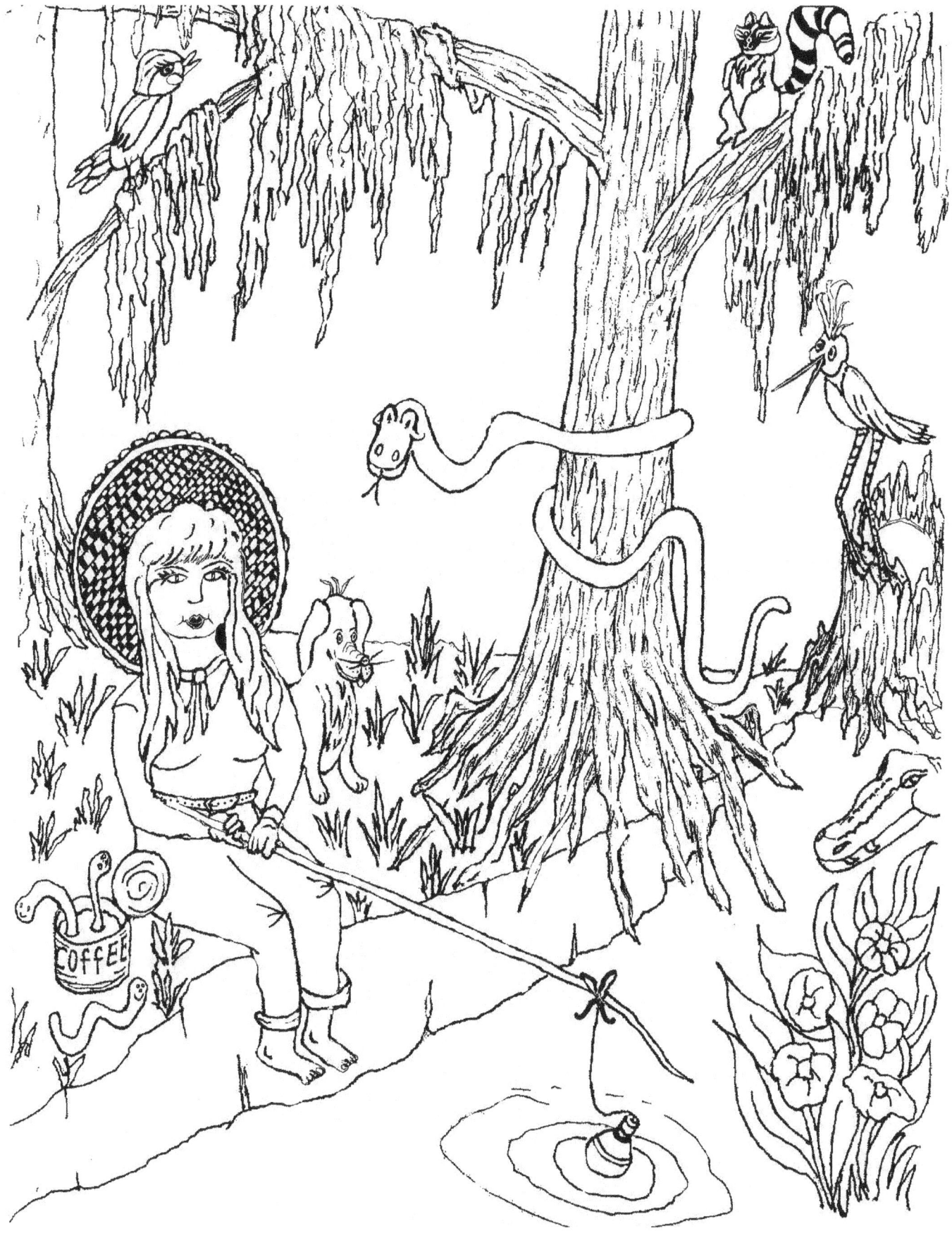

MAMA NET TOLD ME ABOUT MELAND'S DOG. THEY HAD AN OLD DOG NAMED LUCKY. WHAT MADE HIM SO LUCKY, YOU ASK, WAS ALL THE MICE AND BUTTERFLIES, AND TURTLES THAT LOVE HIM. EVERONE KNOWS IF SOMEONE LOVES YOU THEN YOU ARE VERY LUCKY INDEED.

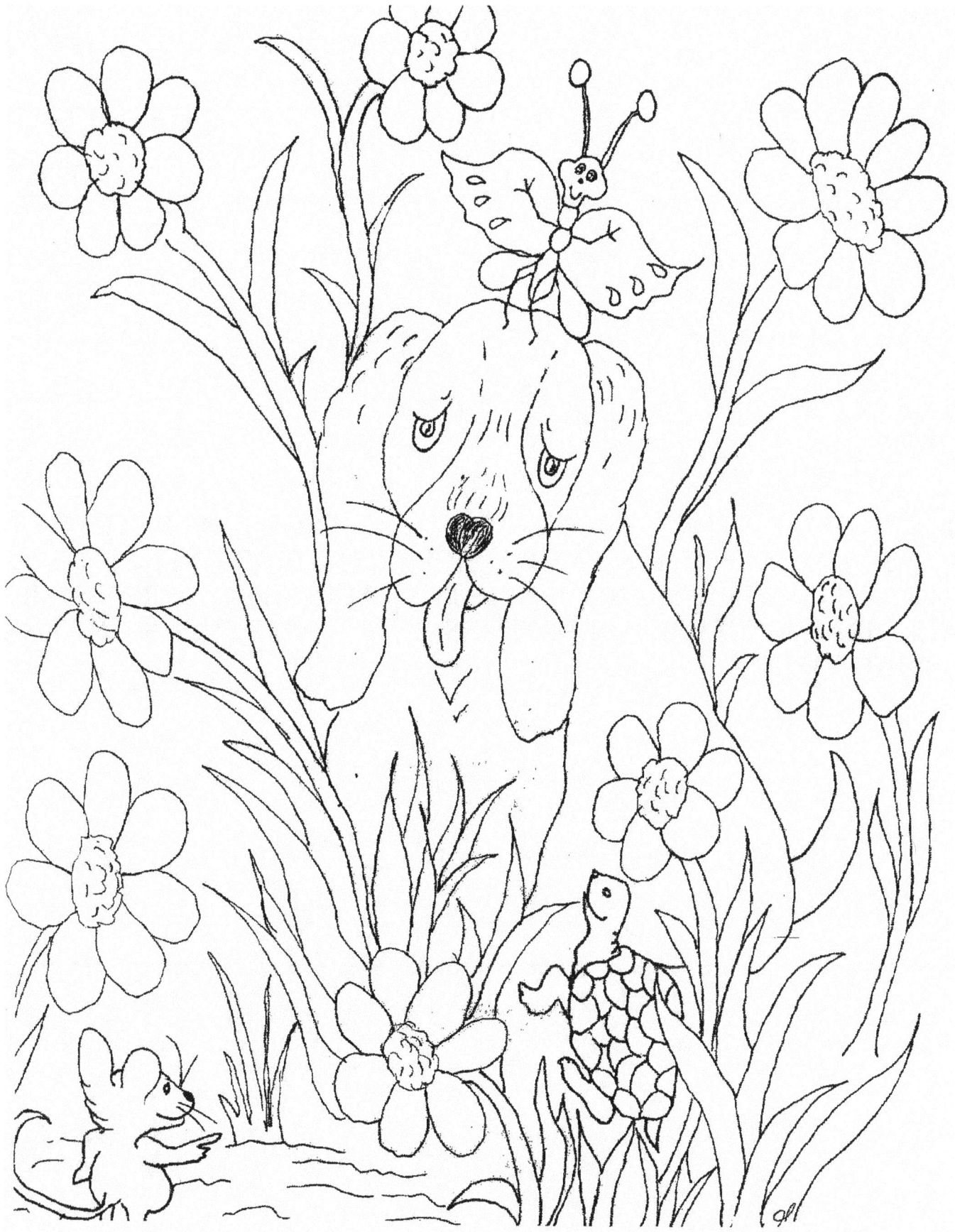

THEN THEY WENT TO TELLING ME ABOUT A BEAUTIFUL PLACE BACK IN THE SWAMP WHERE THE BIRDS NEST IN THE BIG CYPRESS TREES, AND THERE IS SO MANY FLOWERS WHERE ALL THE MOTHER ALLIGATORS LAY THEIR EGGS IN THE SPRING TIME.

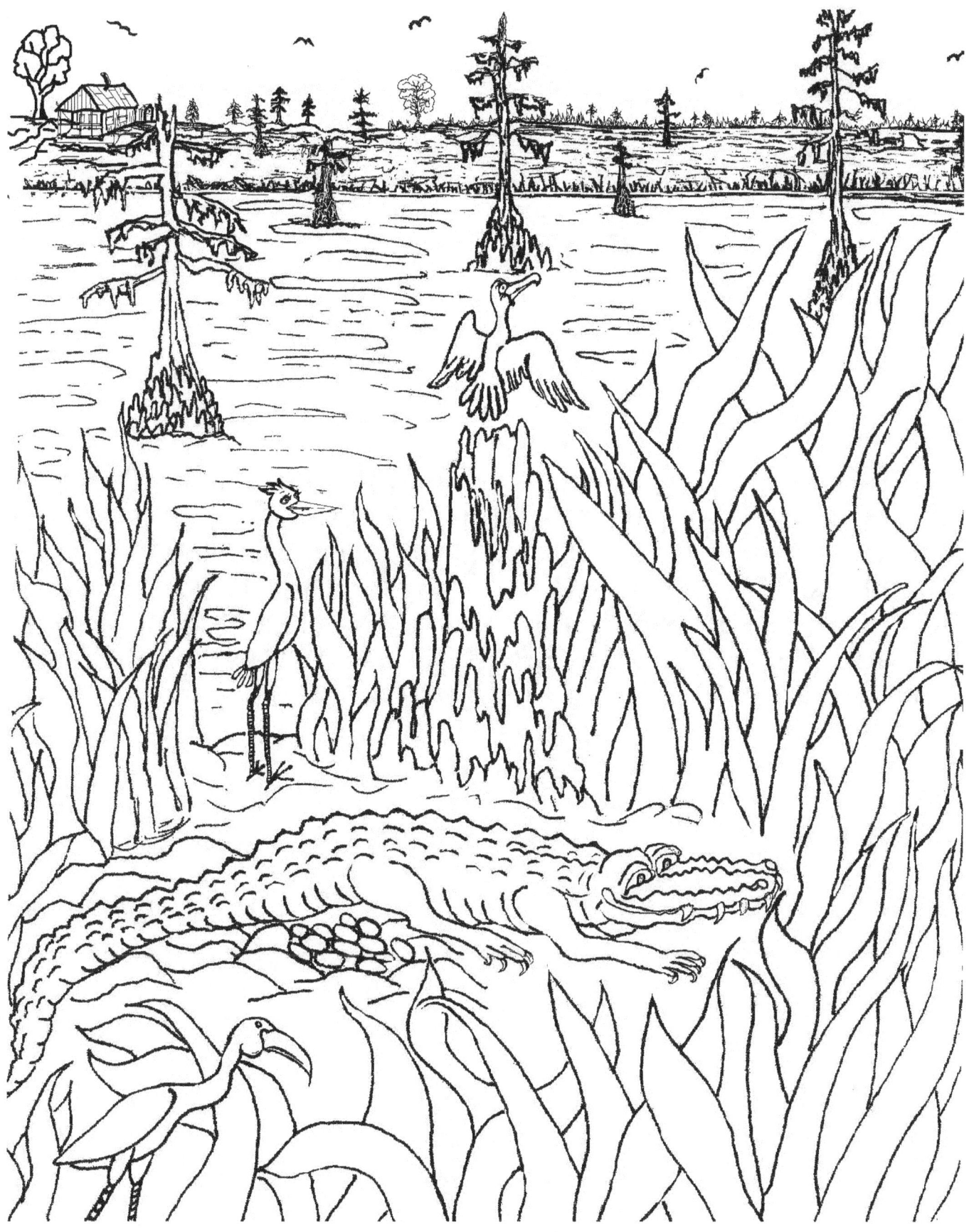

THEN I ASKED, "WHAT ABOUT THIS BLACK WATER?" OH, THE WATER MAY LOOK BLACK IN THE SWAMP, BUT IT IS SWEET AND CLEAN, SO THE CREATURES COME FROM FAR AWAY JUST TO DRINK THE COOL SWEET WATER. THE FOXES NAME IS DOTTY, AND SHE LOVES THE SWAMP WATER THE BEST. SHE THINKS THE WATER HAS MAGIC IN IT AND THAT IS WHY SHE HAS A RED COAT!

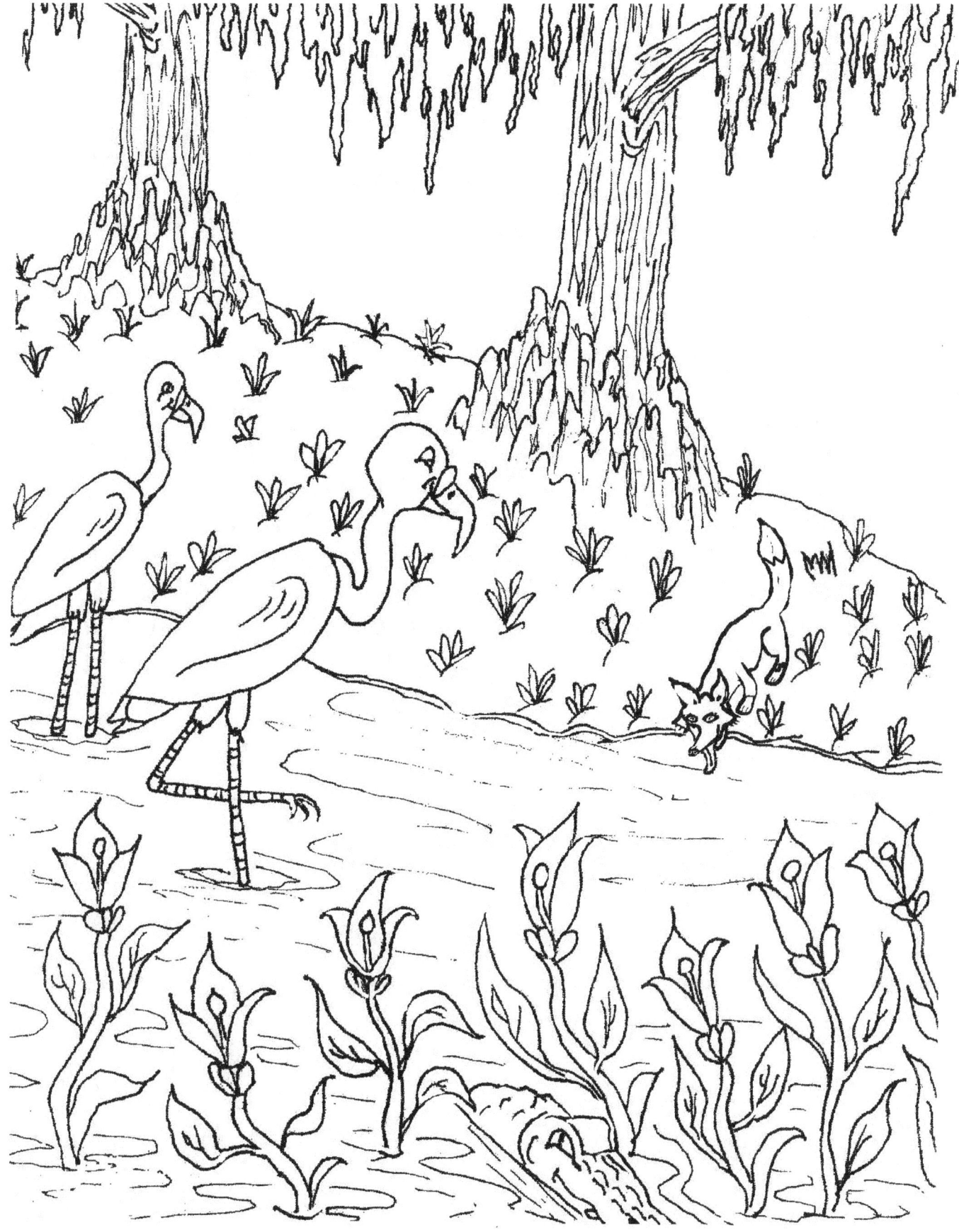

"NOW YOU DO KNOW," ASKED PAPA ODIS, "THAT HERE WE HAVE SUGAR BEARS IN THE SWAMP, TOO?" THEY TOLD ME HIS NAME IS MARK, THE FISHING BEAR, AND HE LOVES TO FISH. HE IS VERY GOOD AT IT, TOO. SUGAR BEAR THINKS THE MAGIC FROM THE DRAGONFLIES IS WHY HE CAN CATCH SO MANY FISH. SO IF YOU SEE DRAGONFLIES AROULD THE WATER, YOU CAN BET FISH ARE IN THAT WATER AND THAT WOULD BE A GOOD PLACE TO GO FISHING.

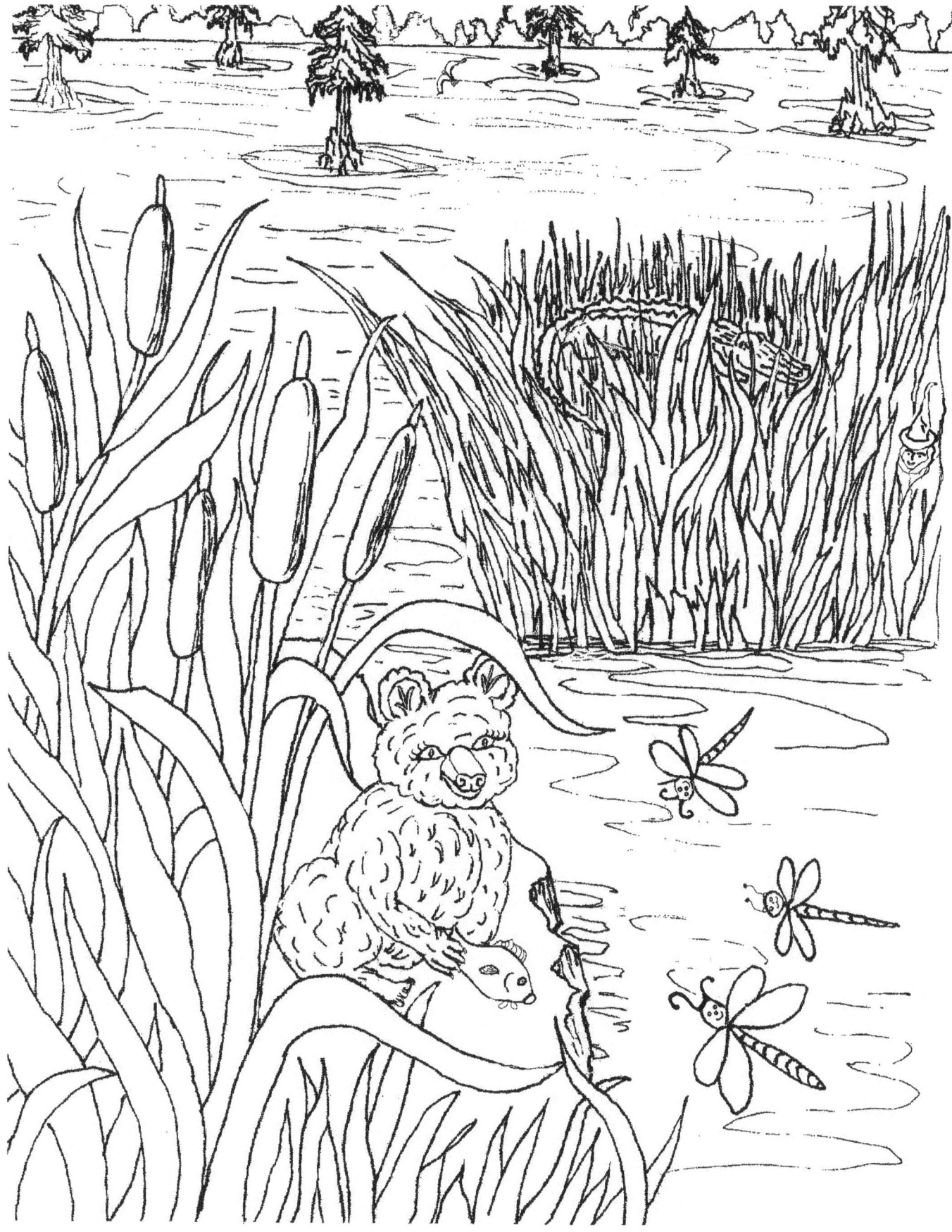

NOW PAPA ODIS WENT TO TELLING ME ABOUT HIS BEST FRIEND WHO IS A HOG NAMED WILD ONION. I ASKED WHY HE WAS NAMED WILD ONION AND HE SAID IT IS BECAUSE HE LOVES TO EAT WILD ONIONS THAT GROW IN THE SWAMP. PAPA ODIS SAID WILD ONION IS THE HAPPIEST HOG WE KNOW AND ALL DAY LONG HE EATS ONIONS, AND WHEN HE IS NOT EATING ONION, THEN HE IS EATING WATER LILIES. PAPA ODIS SAID EVERYONE NEEDS A FRIEND THAT IS HAPPY ALL THE TIME SO THEY CAN HELP YOU BE HAPPY TOO.

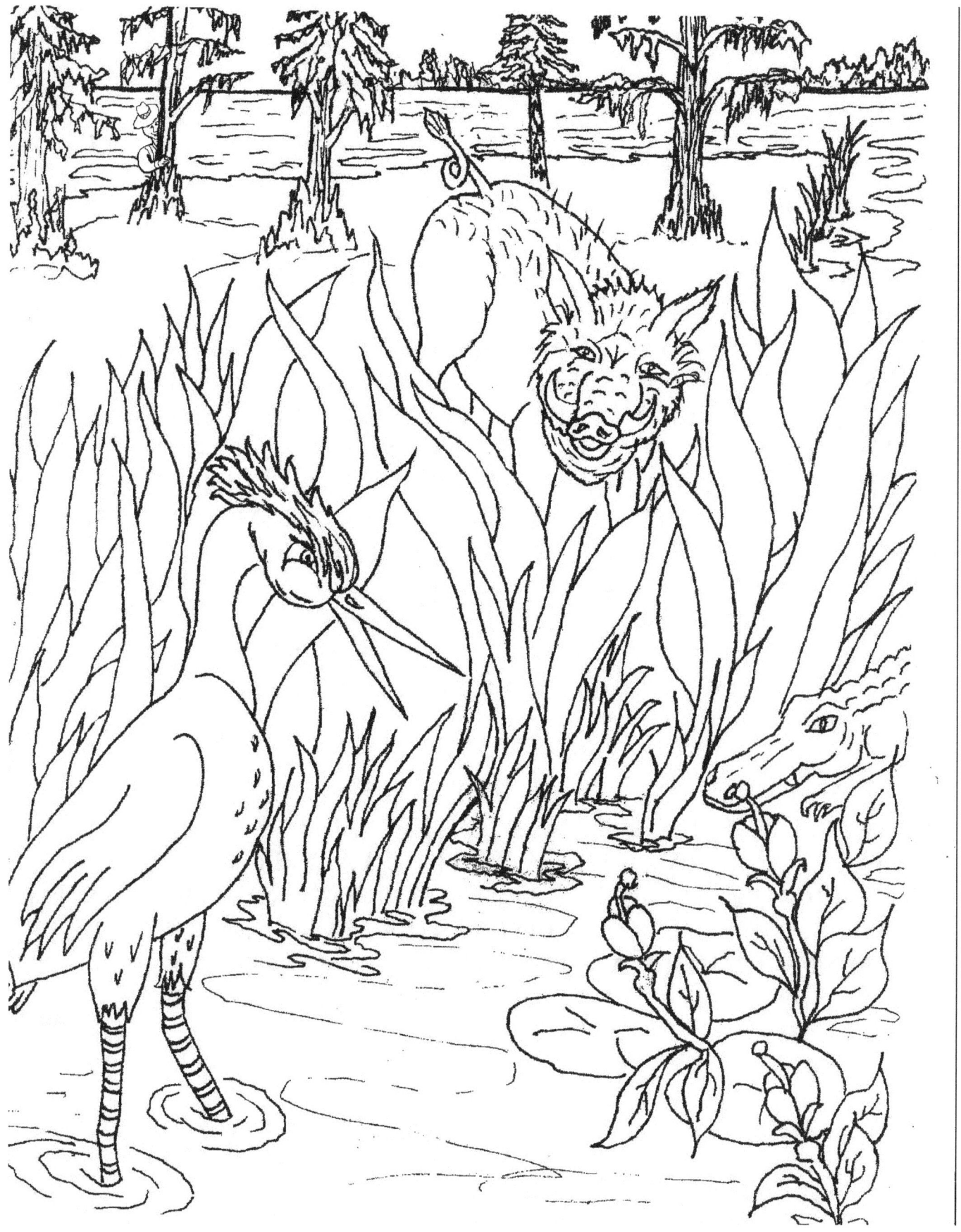

NET'S BEST FRIEND IS A BIG LIGHTENING BUG NAMED BEV, WHICH IS SHORT FOR BEVERLY, BUT SHE LIKED TO BE CALL BEV SO MOST OF THE TIME MAMA NET CALLED HER THAT. BUT SOMETIMES OLD MAMA NET, BEING SO OLD, WOULD FORGET AND CALL HER BEVERLY. NOW LET ME TELL YOU ABOUT BEV AND HER LIGHT. IT IS THE MAGIC LIGHT THAT COMES FROM WITHIN A GOOD SOUL, THE LIGHT THAT IS ALWAYS ON. THIS LIGHT ALWAYS KEEPS MAMA NET ON THE RIGHT PATH. NOW TO HAVE A FRIEND LIKE THAT IS A VERY GOOD THING.

PAPA ODIS SAID THEY HAVE A BIG OLD BULL FROG FRIEND TOO, NAMED NANCY, WITH MAGIC SPOTS ON HER THAT MAKE HER VERY BEAUTIFUL.

MAMA NET HAD ONE FISH FRIEND, AND SHE WAS A VERY SPECIAL MAGIC FISH NAMED JACKIE. WHAT MADE HER SO SPECIAL WAS THAT SHE WAS FRIENDS WITH ALLIGATORS, FROGS, LIGHTENING BUGS, AND ALL THE CREATURES IN THE SWAMP, AND YET SHE COULD USE HER MAGIC SO SUGAR BEARS COULD NOT GET HER AND EAT HER.

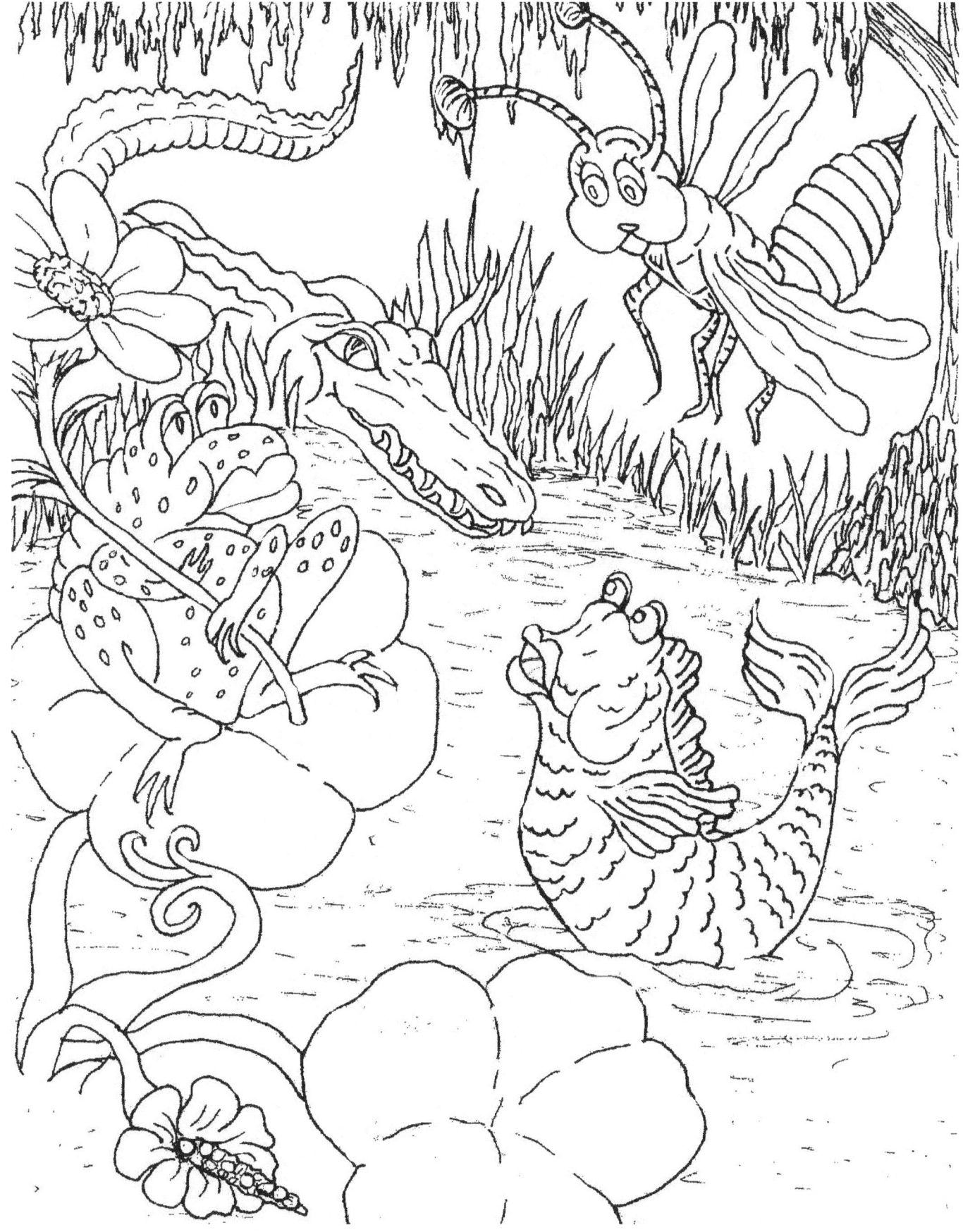

NOW AFTER THE PICNIC WITH PAPA ODIS AND MAMA NET THEY TOLD ME THEY DECIDED TO GET BABY A SUGAR CANE FOR CHRISTMAS, AND THEY SAID GOODBYE TO ME.

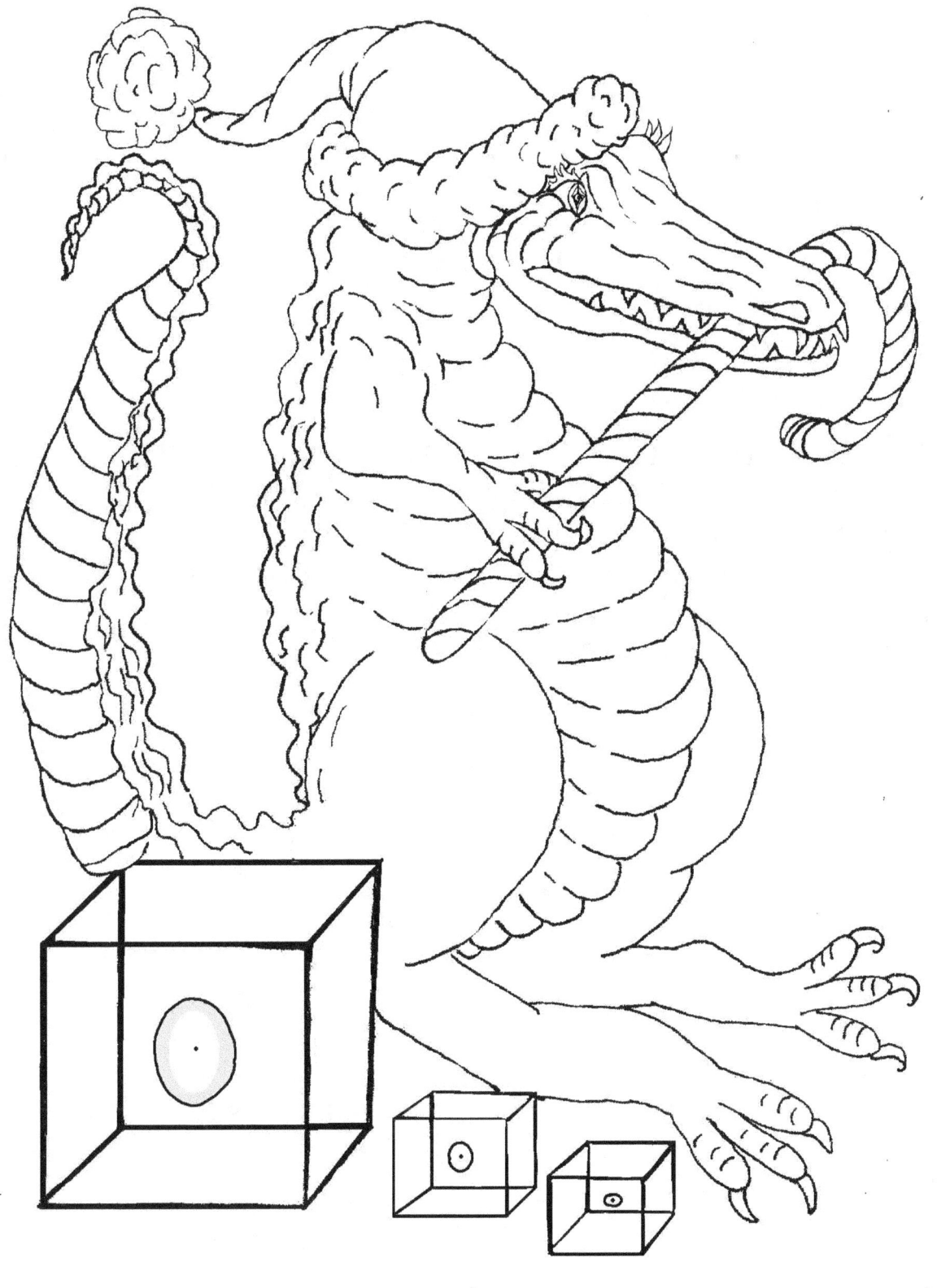

SO, I WAS WALKING OUT OF THE SWAMP AND LOOKED UP AND WHAT I GOT TO SEE WAS PAPA ODIS PULLING SANTAS SLEIGH WITH MAGIC DUST BEING SPRINKLED ALL AROULD FOR THEIR FAMILY AND FRIENDS. IN THE DUST WAS LOVE, HOPE, PEACE, HAPPINESS KINDNESS, AND ALL THE TRUE THINGS WE WOULD LOVE TO HAVE FOR CHISTMAS.

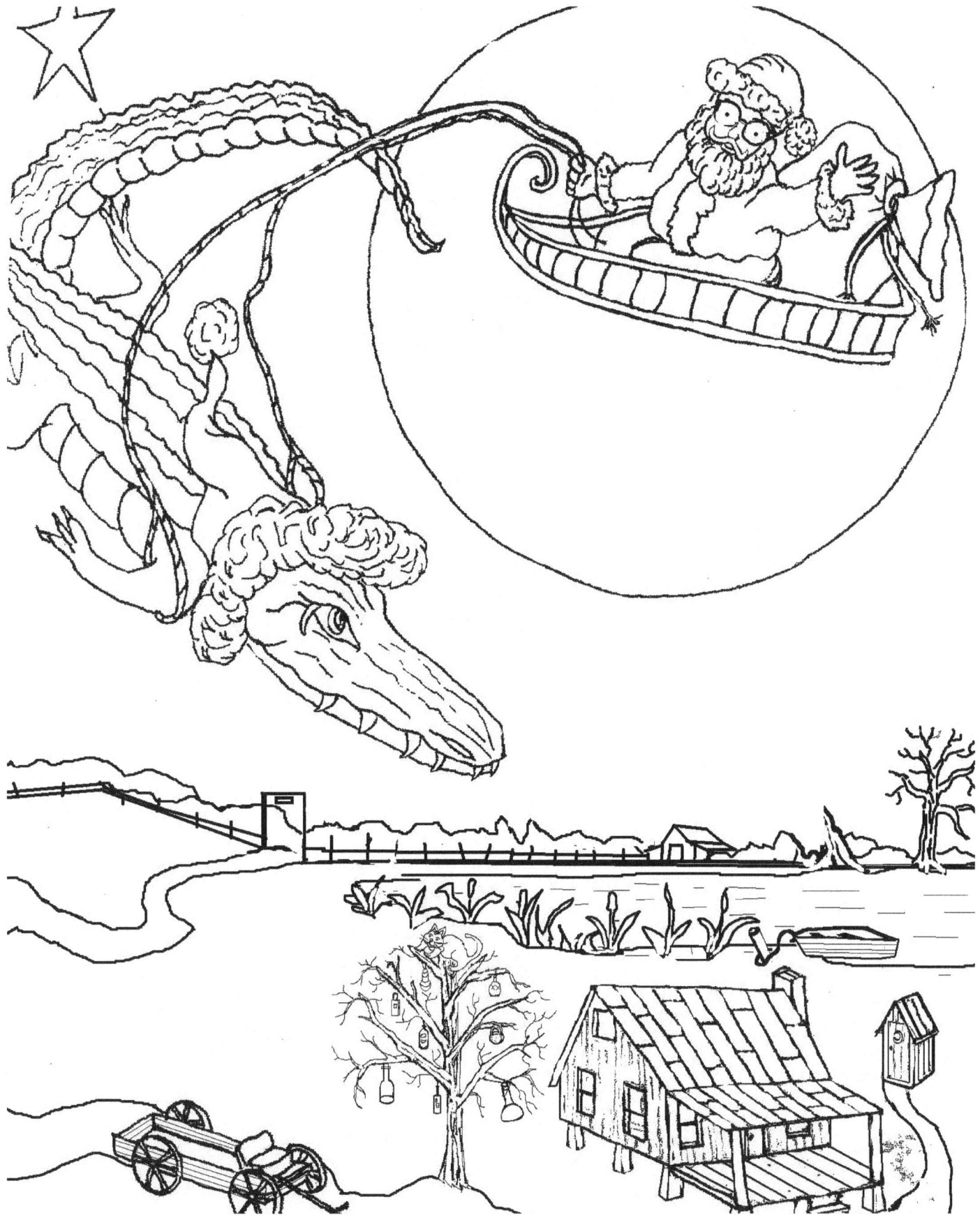

GOODBYE TIL NEXT TIME!

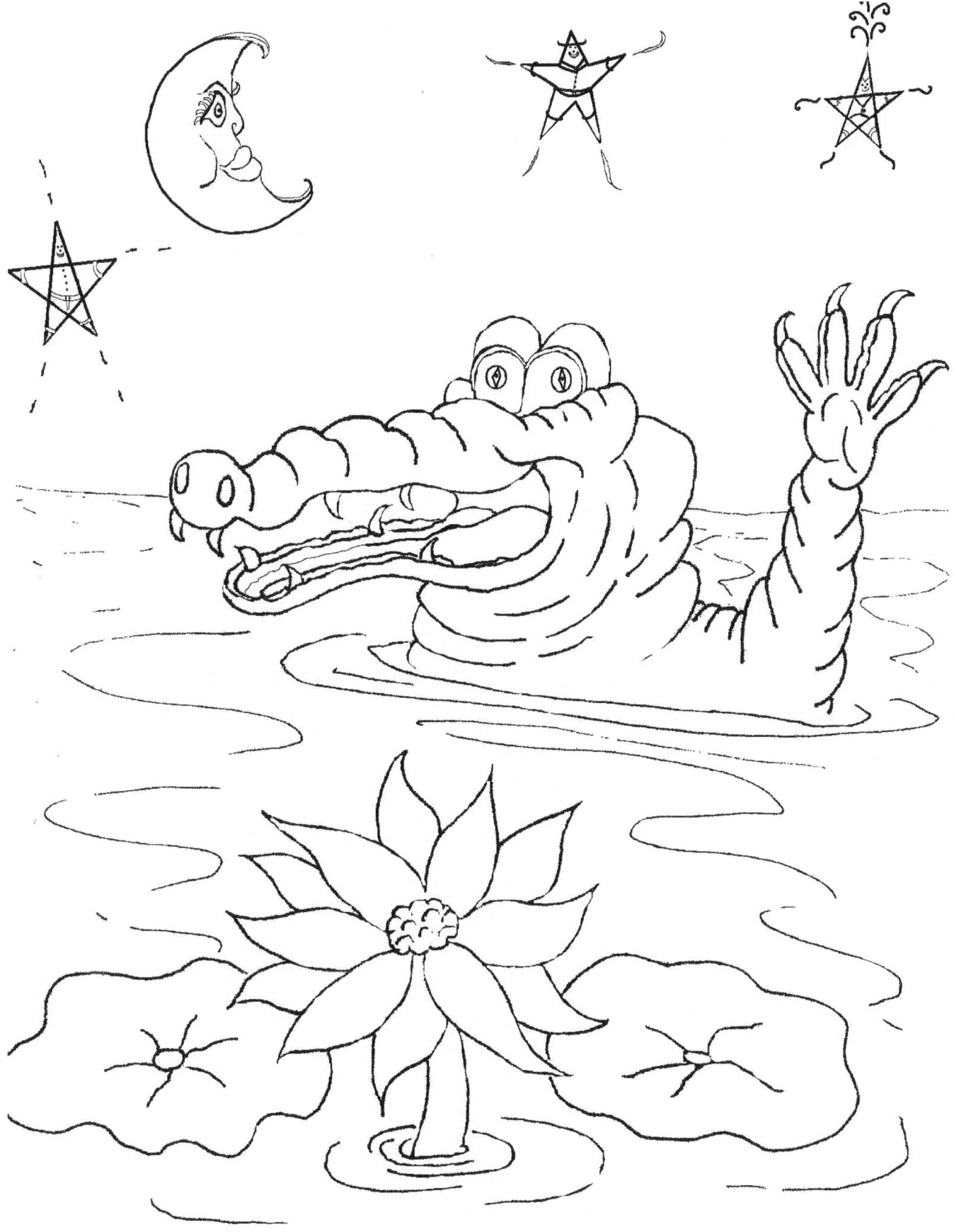

ABOUT THE AUTHOR

NORMA JEAN WAS BORN AND RAISED IN LOUISIANA AND HAS TRAVELED THE COUNTRY IN SEARCH OF ADVENTURE AND MAGIC. THROUGH MUCH OF HER LIFE, SHE HAS CREATED VARIOUS FORMS OF ART IN SCULPTURES, PAINTING, AND SKETCHES WHILE RAISING HER CHILDREN AND LOVING ALL GOD'S CREATURES.